SONGS FROM THE STEPPES:
THE POEMS OF MAKHTUMKULI

Brian Aldiss, OBE, is a fiction and science fiction writer, poet, playwright, critic, memoirist and artist. He was born in Norfolk in 1925. After leaving the army, Aldiss worked as a bookseller, which provided the setting for his first book, *The Brightfount Diaries* (1955). His first published science fiction work was the story 'Criminal Record', which appeared in *Science Fantasy* in 1954. Since then he has written nearly 100 books and over 300 short stories, many of which are being reissued as part of The Brian Aldiss Collection.

Several of Aldiss's books have been adapted for the cinema; his story 'Supertoys Last All Summer Long' was adapted and released as the film *AI* in 2001. Besides his own writing, Brian has edited numerous anthologies of science fiction and fantasy stories, as well as the magazine *SF Horizons*.

Aldiss is a vice-president of the International H. G. Wells Society and in 2000 was given the Damon Knight Memorial Grand Master Award by the Science Fiction Writers of America. Aldiss was awarded the OBE for services to literature in 2005.

T0318044

By the same author from The Friday Project

BRIAN ALDISS

SONGS FROM THE STEPPES: THE POEMS OF MAKHTUMKULI

The Friday Project
An imprint of HarperCollins*Publishers*
77–85 Fulham Palace Road,
Hammersmith, London W6 8JB

www.harpercollins.co.uk

This paperback edition 2014
First published: The Society of Friends of Makhtumkuli, 1995
1

A catalogue record for this book is
available from the British Library

ISBN: 978-0-00-748275-7

Find out more about HarperCollins and the environment at
www.harpercollins.co.uk/green

Introduction to the 2014 Edition

Make no mistake, this slender volume represents a vital segment of my life.

A writer inevitably sends out messages into the blue; occasionally an unexpected response arrives in the lap of the computer.

So it was that I first heard from Dr Youssef Azemoun. Azemoun worked in an obscure division of the BBC. He came from Turkmenistan, or, as he put it, 'I was born on the south side of a river, and so I was a Muslim. Had I been born on the north side of that river, I would have been a Communist.'

He was a jolly man, and a clever one. He played a silver flute. It happened that he and his wife were about to hold a party. I was invited to it.

The Azemouns lived in Reading, in a house full of light, cooking, music and other Muslims.

I had a splendid time – so much so, indeed, that soon Youssef was inviting me to accompany him and his wife on a visit to Turkmenistan, Turkmenistan the Distant! The Unknown! Of course I said yes.

So I found myself in Ashkabad, the capital city – indeed, almost Turkmenistan's only city, since much of the country is smothered by the Karakum, the great red desert. Its seaport to the west is set on the coast of the Caspian. Some of the capital's streets are surprisingly attractive, with little rivulets twinkling along beside their pavements, helping to cool the day's Central Asian temperatures. When the Russians possessed the state, a violent earthquake occurred. The current elegance is owed to Russian designers, who repaired the damage. A similar inheritance is the generosity with which male Muslims drink vodka. It makes one feel at home.

As I had spent a year in Jugoslavia as a substitute for Burma and Sumatra, now Turkmenistan served as a substitute for Jugoslavia – 'Jugland', as we called it. Thus I found myself in one of the city's best hotels – which I christened 'The Nadir'. I slept on a mattress laid over an old green door, supported by empty orange crates. Never have I slept so deeply or so well. And there was a radio, on which one could tune to Moscow One or Moscow Two. I won't go into the toilet facilities.

Days tended towards the intellectual. I gave a lecture. Of the five states made free of Russian possession in 1991, each chose a figurehead to represent them. Most chose warriors, Genghis Khan among them. But Turkmenistan had chosen a poet, the great Makhtumkuli. It was as if, on the top of our Nelson Monument in Trafalgar Square we had placed – not the brave Horatio but – Algernon Charles Swinburne.

Connected with the university was a group of Indian Muslims, taking refuge from newly freed Hindu India. Rather touchingly, I found them pleased, indeed delighted, to meet me. Most of them spoke good clear English, which needed exercise. I wonder, most likely they are still there, and reading Makhtumkuli. But I shall never again be in Ashkabad.

Youssef had once upon a time been Minister of Culture. He had become so popular that the president had sacked him. Now there we were, planning an English edition of the poems of their honoured poet. Youssef would translate, but who do you think would versify …

So, back at home in my comfortable house on Boars Hill I set to work with the results you see before you.

I worked all summer long. Of course I never asked for or received a penny for my labours. This was a way of thanking Youssef for that absorbing trip, and for his splendid friendship. And, of course, of seeing if I could do it.

Be friendly to these verses, please. I did my best for them over that long summer …

Brian Aldiss
Oxford, 2014

CONTENTS

Introduction to the 1995 Edition

Very little is known in the West about the Turkmens, their language and their literature. The Turkmen national poet Makhtumkuli Feraghy, was introduced to the Western literary world last century after the translation into English of three of his 'songs' by Alexander Chodzko in 1842 in London, and the publication of thirty poems in Turkmen with German translations by the Hungarian scholar Vambery, who carried out research into the poet's life during his excursion to Central Asia last century. However, apart from the recent translation of a number of his poems into French, little attention has been paid to Makhtumkuli since.

Turkmen literature assumed its full identity after the emergence of Makhtumkuli in the 18th century. The simple yet profound quality of his poems has, over two centuries, dominated the minds of not only the Turkmens, but all Turkic peoples living in the vast region from the Oxus to the Transcaucasus. Berdak, a Karakalpak classical poet, said: 'I worship Makhtumkuli's every word.' Vambery wrote that the poems of Makhtumkuli were second to the Koran among the Turkmen people. To many Makhtumkuli is so revered that he is something more than a poet – a saint perhaps. He is a poet of the highest spiritual dimensions. He has written on a variety of themes – mystical, lyrical, religious, social, patriotic and others which make his poems appeal to various strata among the Turkmens and other peoples. This quality made Makhtumkuli a national poet even in his own time. V.V. Bartold, a distinguished Russian Orientalist, wrote: 'Makhtumkuli, who is a Gokleng, is the national poet of the Turkmens, including the Turkmens of Stavropol ...' (Sochineniya, vol. 2, p614, 1963), '... the only people among the Turkic peoples who have a national poet are the Turkmens.' (Ibid, vol. 5, p187, 1968).

Archives yield very little information about Makhtumkuli. What we know about him comes above all from his own poems and from the wealth of popular stories. Vambery provided valuable information by interviewing a Turkmen religious figure called Gyzyl Akhun last century. Interviews with Gara Ishan, a descendant of the father of Makhtumkuli of the sixth generation, who died at the age of 53 in 1992, are also useful. He gave a vivid account of previous interviews with elders of the Gokleng tribe and others. The information he provided is regarded as valuable and reliable.

The exact date and place of birth of Makhtumkuli are not known. He is believed to have been born in 1733. He was the third son of Dowletmamet Azadi, who is also known as Garry Molla (1700–1765). Azadi was a great poet, a writer, scholar and author of several books. Makhtumkuli was named after his grandfather, Makhtumkuli Yonachy (1654–1720). He belonged to the Gyshyklar clan of the Gerkez division of the Gokleng tribe of the Turkmens. In a poem about the weight of the chains on his legs when he was taken captive, he introduces himself to his captors and thereby to his readers:

Tell those who enquire about me
That I am a Gerkez, I hail from Etrek and my name is Makhtumkuli

Makhtumkuli's father was his first teacher and mentor. His father sent the young Makhtumkuli to a teacher called Niyaz

Salih. During his studies Makhtumkuli also acquired the skills of a silversmith and a saddler. He studied in a Madrassah (religious school) called Idris Baba; he continued his education in Bukhara and finished it at the Shir Gazi Madrassah in Khiva where his talent was recognised and he was appointed a 'khalifa', a substitute teacher. He mastered classical Arabic, Persian and Turkic languages and literatures beside his religious education. He returned home and began teaching at his village while plying the craft of a silversmith. One story supported by a poem he wrote entitled 'Defy the Fiend!' depicts him as both a craftsman and a man who attaches importance to moral values. A beautiful young lady orders Makhtumkuli to make a silver artefact. When the object is ready the young woman tries to avoid payment by seducing him. Makhtumkuli manages to resist her charms and she has to give up the attempt. He says:

> Your lust shouts, 'Do it! Seize it for relief!'
> But conscience whispers, 'No – God sees a thief.'
> Though you are blind, He watches you with grief:
> Forget your impulse, let shame keep its lair.

According to another story Makhtumkuli says to the woman (or to himself in some versions): 'Place your hand on this ember, and if you can bear its heat, we may establish a friendship. If not stay away!'. This story is confirmed by the last stanza of the same poem:

> When Satan says, 'It's sweet – forget your soul!',
> God says 'Defy the Fiend, stay in control!'
> So Makhtumkuli, seize the blazing coal:
> Then go and do it – if pain you can bear!

His true love lay with Mengli (meaning a girl with a beauty spot), whose real name is said to be Yangybeg. She was a handsome

3

dark-haired girl from the Gyshyklar clan of the Goklengs. She was beautiful and literate. Impressed by her beauty and intelligence, Makhtumkuli wanted to marry Mengli, but while he was away studying, she was forcibly married to someone else, and Makhtumkuli was left with a broken heart from which he perhaps never recovered.

According to a story told by Gara Ishan, Makhtumkuli later saw Mengli lying dead. 'The Nightingale', one of his poems about his separation from Mengli, expresses his desperation. This poem has become the lyric of one of the most popular Turkmen folk songs:

> I'm a nightingale. Here's my sad song
> From my Garden of roses. Now I've begun.
> See the tears in my eyes? There they belong.
> What pleasure in life when loving is done?

According to one account he was married to the wife of his elder brother, who had disappeared. This cannot be true, because the body of his brother was never recovered. The poem 'Abdulla Absent' about the disappearance of Makhtumkuli's brother, says that Abdulla went on a journey and did not come back. According to another story, he was married to a certain Akgyz who some people assume was his sister-in-law. Whoever his wife may have been, it seems that he did not have a happy married life. In 'Marrying', a satirical poem, he complains about marriage and tries to dissuade his readers. He says: 'If you aspire to become an old ass, Go and get married!' However, he was against bigamy although it was permitted. In another satirical poem about men with two wives, entitled 'Two Wives', he portrays their disastrous family life and ridicules them as the third woman in the family:

> If he can't coax her out of all such games
> Or call the pair of them by pretty names –

Well, dolts like that are scarcely proper men!
So wives plus husband rightly make – three dames!

He ends his poem by counselling his readers that marriage should
be based on understanding:

O Makhtumkuli, let's not that way sink!
Better wed once with understanding …

Makhtumkuli had two sons. One of them, Sary, died when he was
seven years old, and the other son, Ibrahim, died at the age of ten.
The loss of both his sons left a deep and indelible mark on his
poetic soul. In his poem 'Loss', which is one of his most effective
elegies, he depicts the reaction of certain birds and animals to the
loss of their young and compares his state of mind with that of
the birds and animals. He ends the poem thus:

How can we bear the pangs of final parting,
Though Death may steal upon us while we sleep?
Even if Makhtumkuli's son were nothing but
A cub, what then? What should he do all day but weep?

Makhtumkuli was a Sufi. He sought the blessing of a Sufi leader
or sage. The Sufi, said to be called Shah Gurbat, was told that a
poet who was a Turkmen wished to see him. He said he did not
want to see a poet who talked nonsense. Makhtumkuli then wrote
his famous poem 'I Took Up My Pen' which gives an insight into
his enormous literary learning. He likened the Sufi to 'a young
hawk, (with) feathers still ungrown.' According to a story the Sufi
travelled a long way to meet Makhtumkuli and apologise.

Makhtumkuli's elegy about his father, 'My Father', gives a good
picture of a man of virtue who had influenced him profoundly
and whom he regarded as his Kaaba (the sacred Muslim shrine in
Mecca). The loss of his father made him suffer spiritually as well

as emotionally; it deprived him of a spiritual intimacy. Perhaps as a Sufi he needed this separation to reach his perfection, or his spiritual maturity:

> Love caught fire within my heart, and burned and blazed.
> Smoke whirling in the wind whipped me like something crazed.
> Fate caught me, spinning me upon its wheel.
> Who came to see me through the eyes of real desire?
> Separation was a storm – both flood and fire.
>
> 'The Pains of Love'

Separation makes a man burn and turn into ashes; in other words, helps a man to be 'annihilated in God':

> O, hopeful slave to the beloved's charms, whereby
> I lost my heart! A songbird of sweet tongues was I –
> Encaged! But separation scorched my soul.
> Then yearning burned me up, to ash was turned my mind.
> And Makhtumkuli's life was tossed upon the wind.
>
> 'The Pains of Love'

The words 'pain' and 'burning' proliferate in some of Makhtumkuli's poems, because some Sufis summarise their life in three words – being raw, becoming mature (by the fire of tribulations) and being burnt (and turning to ashes).

Makhtumkuli attached great importance to the Truth and the concept of a perfect man, as a Sufi would do. However, the human suffering and social injustice which he witnessed around himself made him pay attention to worldly matters too. He became more interested in the concept of the happiness of his people. Even in his mystic poems like 'The Riddle: A Vision' he defends justice, moral values and the oppressed. Viewing life from the point of view of human morality became part and parcel of his sense of humanity and his love for people. It is these feelings that make it impossible

6

for him to become reconciled to the corruption and injustice of society. In the following lines he depicts the position of the poor:

> A poor man goes barefoot, showing his need.
> At meetings they will seat him low indeed,
> While if he rides a horse it's called an ass –
> A rich man's ass, of course, is called a steed!
>
> 'Be Not Poor!'

He cannot do much to help the poor, who are despised even by their own close relatives, but encourages them that some day – even if that day might be Judgement Day – they will be strong:

> Oppressors then will have to play the moke –
> The poor, of course, will be the forest lion.
>
> 'Perfection'

He harshly criticises the oppressor and corrupt people of society:

> Sultans now laugh at justice in eclipse.
> These derelictions spell apocalypse,
> When farthings buy a mufti's best decree
> And tyrants die with no prayer on their lips.
>
> 'An Age without Morality'

In the poem 'Everything Openly' Makhtumkuli describes the beauty of Central Asia, where the seasons are pronounced and the steppes produce a fine display of colours. In what can be regarded as one of his nature poems, Makhtumkuli compares the regrowing of plants to resurrection.

> When Nawruz falls, the world takes colour – openly:
> Clouds cry aloud, mountains gather haze – openly:
> Even the lifeless come to life – breathing openly:

7

Plants, before unseen, grow up and blossom – openly:
All creatures benefit or do us harm – openly:
They breed their kind and stealthily go by – openly:
Birds open beaks and sing when summer comes – openly.

He suffered a tragic personal and family life amid endemic tribal conflicts which intensified in the 18th century as the Turkmens became fragmented into smaller groups. This made it easy for the neighbouring rulers and khans to invade and plunder the Turkmen territory. It was during such an invasion that Makhtumkuli lost the fruit of years of hard and devoted work when the contents of his house, including his manuscripts, were taken away on camels. It is said that Makhtumkuli saw the camel carrying his manuscripts slip, hurling the manuscripts into the river Etrek, thus making the river an enemy of the poet.

The poem 'Making My Dear Life Lost' recounts this sad event:

Making my dear life lost to all that's good,
An evil fate wrought awesome sacrilege,
Hurling the books I'd written to the flood,
To leave me bookless with my grief and rage.

It is evident from some of his poems that Makhtumkuli himself was taken captive. In the poem 'The Twelve Imams' the poet describes the virtues of each of the Twelve Imams and asks for forgiveness by invoking the sacred memory of every one. According to one account, Makhtumkuli, his mother and his brother-in-law were seized by a Shiite ruler in Mashhad, a holy town in Iran, home of the shrine of Imam Riza, the eighth Imam. It is related that the ruler released the mother and told her that she could take one of the men with her. She asked for the release of her son-in-law rather than Makhtumkuli. Later, when asked why she had done so, she replied that Makhtumkuli was a poet and a master of words, and would be able to find a way out.

And indeed he was set free after reciting his poem 'The Twelve Imams', pleading for forgiveness.

'When The Sun Drives Its Daggers' was written when a poor young man told Makhtumkuli that he was in love with the daughter of a rich man, but could not have her hand. Makhtumkuli said in this poem 'Jackals eat the finest melons'. The young man was initially offended, but accepted the reality after reading the whole poem more carefully. Makhtumkuli wrote some other poems for other people to help them express their feelings.

Makhtumkuli was a man concerned with the welfare of his people. There are tales which say that he personally resolved disputes between various tribes. He believed that the whole tragedy of the Turkmens was due to the quarrels and disunity among the tribes. In some of his poems he warns his people against internecine strife. Having realised the dangers of tribalism, in his poem 'Exhortation In Time Of Trouble', he calls on the Turkmen tribes by their names, to unite into a single national state, thus becoming the first Turkmen poet to introduce such a political theme into Turkmen literature. He says:

If Turkmens would only tighten the Belt of Determination
They could drink the Red Sea in their strength.
So let the tribes of Teke, Yomut, Gokleng, Yazir, and Alili
Unite into one proud nation.

According to widespread stories, Makhtumkuli died as a result of the unbearable oppression of sad experiences in his old age, aggravated by his distress at the tribal hostility which had caused him so much suffering. The date of his death is not known, but it is thought to be towards the end of the 18th century or the beginning of the 19th century. Before his death he sat at his open door to look for the last time at the splendour of the mountains which had been so much a part of his life. Here is how the poem 'When I Cease To Be' ends:

Whoever lives will soon in graves have lain;
Says Makhtumkuli, death devours all sins.
The sky remains, while earth in orbit spins.
The sun will rise and set, moon wax and wane …

There are over a hundred manuscripts of Makhtumkuli's collected poems in Turkmenistan, and many others in Iran, Afghanistan and other places; there is one manuscript of Makhtumkuli's poems at the British Library which also has poems by other Turkmen classical poets. None of these manuscripts are complete. The original manuscript of the author has never been discovered. A large manuscript which is believed to belong to Makhtumkuli was seen at the turn of this century, once in a village in northern Iran and another time in Garry Gala in Turkmenistan, but it has not been seen since. Under the Soviet system, people were persecuted for having books with Arabic script in their homes since they were regarded as religious. Many destroyed or buried old manuscripts or even hung them in old wells. Some were discovered after Perestroika, but many had already disappeared and the poet's own manuscript might be among them. Collections of poems of Makhtumkuli from these manuscripts were published several times in Turkmenistan in the Soviet period, but religious poems were excluded from them. Only after Perestroika did these poems begin to appear in Turkmen literary journals. A collection of 'Unpublished Poems Of Makhtumkuli' called 'Bagyshla Bizni', meaning 'Forgive Us' which is the title of the poem 'The Twelve Imams', was published in 1990 and consisted of religious poems including 'When Judgement Day Comes' and 'Dawn Is The Time' both of which feature in 'Songs From The Steppes'.

Most of the manuscripts begin with the poem 'Revelation', the first version of which was written by Makhtumkuli when he was nine years old. He developed it later. There are many incompatibilities in the text in various manuscripts. Makhtumkuli must have revised the poem a number of times. Gara Ishan once said that when Makhtumkuli was about nine years old, his family went to a funeral leaving him at home sleeping. A sack of grain fell on him when he was asleep. He was dreaming. When he woke up his mouth was foaming and this is mentioned in the poem. (There is a striking similarity between parts of this poem (and another poem 'The Riddle: A Vision') and a poem by Pushkin called 'The Prophet'. A Russian scholar, Bertels, and a Turkmen scholar, Zilikha Mukhammedova have compared the poems.) Makhtumkuli had a great love for his mother tongue, and he brings out the richness and beauty of the Turkmen language. He made ingenious use of the everyday language of the people, at a time when the Turkmen language was under the influence of Chaghatay, the stilted written language of culture in use throughout Central Asia. He broke the barrier between the literary language before him and the common language of the people, transforming the 18th century literary language and making it accessible to the people. He also used the wealth of Turkmen folklore with some skill. Avoiding verbiage he expressed his ideas in as few words as possible, and applied proverbs whenever appropriate. Many of his verses have themselves turned into proverbs, which sometimes makes it difficult to distinguish real proverbs from Makhtumkuli's inventions. His clarity and simplicity make his striking use of imagery all the more effective.

He wrote some poems in the classical forms, but most of them use the popular form 'qoshuk'. Qoshuks are poems consisting of quatrains with lines of eight or eleven (or occasionally seven) syllables. This form of poem, lucidly written and rooted in folklore, creates a musicality which suits Turkmen folk music and makes it easily understood and eagerly taken up by 'Baghsys', the folk singers. This is one of the reasons why his poems have spread over a vast area from Central Asia to the Caucasus. His qoshuks generally have the rhyming scheme of A, B, C, B in the first stanza and C, C, C, B and D, D, D, B and so on in the remaining stanzas.

Being a representative of oral tradition Makhtumkuli, like others of his kind in Eastern literature, needed to ensure that he was distinguished from his imitators. This he did by incorporating the trope of addressing himself in the last stanza of every poem. It served as a kind of signature or verification of the poem's authenticity:

O Makhtumkuli, worlds float in your thought
When you were young you only cared for sport:
Now you are thirty and you see more plain;
Those tears that fall announce your sad report.

'Dawn Is The Time'

The first poet to introduce political themes, social criticism and even new forms into Turkmen literature, Makhtumkuli wrote on an enormous variety of subjects which appeal to various strata of Turkmen and other Turkic peoples. For this reason some see Makhtumkuli as a spiritual leader and a teacher, others as a patriot and a guide leading his people to happiness. To the Turkmens he is 'Magtymguly, Bagtyng guly' – the bestower of Happiness.

Y. AZEMOUN

The Revelation

Hark, then, how one night, when I sleeping lay
Four horsemen came. 'Arise, young lad!' said they,
'For who but the Enlightened Ones draw nigh –
And you may see them straightaway.'

Beholding those four riders, I declare
My heart burned with a joyance near despair –
Transfixed I stood. Two holy madmen near
Said, 'Haste, my son, and go thou there.'

The madmen led me forward by the hand
Away from where I lingered, near unmanned.
One gave a gesture. 'Keep vigil,' he said;
The other mouthed a single 'Stand!'

We waited. Came two saints with eyes ashine
With unshed tears, and prayers to the Divine.
Came six more men on foot, crying, 'He's here,
The Man! With his your gaze entwine!'

Came four more horsemen dressed in green, on jet
Black stallions, green-reined. When all were met,

Said they, 'The circle is too small and we
Are many – set it wider yet.'

Came sixty other riders then, apace:
All greet each other quickly, face-to-face,
'Salaam aleykum, brethren!' Then, 'Waste not
One hour, press on to yon great place!'

They saddled me to horse. We rode along
To that great meeting place where, thousands strong,
Men gathered sat. I held back in my awe.
'Son,' said they, 'Come now, join the throng'.

Ali – no less! – took hold my hand thereat,
Dragged up a palliasse whereon I sat,
And poured I knew not what upon my head:
'This is Time Passing – drink of that!'

I begged old Haidar then name so-and-so.
'Why, that's the Prophet, dear to all below,
That's Eslim Hoja, there's Baba Zuryat.
Veys-al-Karani you should know.'

'That's Bahauddin, also Enlightened, there
Near Zengi Baba, famed beyond compare.
And next, close-knit, the Four Companions stand.
Speak, youth – All your desires lay bare.'

Two young sheikhs also present kindly said,
'The thirty prophets by companions led –
By number also thirty – have arrived.
Pour blessings on this young man's head.'

Now, lo, the Prophet calls, 'Omar, Osman,
Eslim Hoja, Great Ali – if you can,
With Baba Salman, Abu Bakr Siddiq,
Wishes fulfil of this young man.'

Eslim and Baba Salman brought an urn,
Into the liquid bade the cup return.
I swooning lay. They ordered me to view
All things of earth and Heaven's concern.

So I became a gale! – And to the tall
Blue vault of Heaven and the deepest pall
Of earth did blow! 'Now go and see',
Said they, 'Yourself behold the Lord of All.'

Whatever thing I thought about was mine
And he was everything I saw, divine.
In sleep I blessed his spittle on my cheek.
'Now rise', they called, 'Arise and shine!'

Then spake the Prophet, 'Brethren of acclaim,
Pour out your blessings on this young man's name',
And to the horsemen four an order gave
To take me back from whence I came.

This beardless youth awoke. His eyes ope wide
To think what wondrous things he had espied.
Bathing his fevered brow he heard them say,
Fading, 'May God be e'er your guide'.

The Riddle: A Vision

Recalling all my sins, I tore my clothes.
Oh, to be lamenting in the morning!
Countless my tears! Sorrow
Possessed me, day or night or dawning.

My love of life had withered like a flower.
I looked up to the night sky in its pallor,
Crying my soul was dead.
I cried aloud to Jesus and to Allah.

A vision then! The stars like honey ran
And I became an infant unattired
As three Enlightened ones
Appeared, approaching me. My thought expired …

One dressed in green, one white, one green again.
One touched me on the chest, one with a sword
Split my sad heart in twain.
One with his mouth on mine spake, 'Hear the Lord!'

Speechless, I caught the words, 'Let sorrow speak,
You mortal'. Love then, purging all suspicion,

Prompted a riddle from me:
My riddled life requiring exposition.

One tall, one small, and one diminutive,
Serene yet smiling then, they Three attended.
'Foolish or wise,' one said,
'A man may find his life's dilemma mended.'

Straightway, I asked, 'What's heavier than sky,
Wider than earth, richer than sea, than stone
More hard, than fire more hot.
Colder than ice – and to the soul alone

More poisonous than hemlock?' Answering,
They said, 'False accusations have more weight
Than sky. Wider than the world
Are fine just words. Harder than stone or slate

The heart of a hypocrite, while like vast seas
Are those who love. The favours of the mean
Chill more than ice. Oppressed,
The poor shed tears that poison souls unseen.'

Thus was my riddle laid to rest. I rose
Up from the dust and bowed to kiss their hands.
I could not say a word.
What's man, to think he ever understands?

Fading away, the Three with one voice said,
'Be wise, O Makhtumkuli'. Still I get
In dreams a doubt that asks,
Why is the world so filled with riddles yet?

The Cup Of Truth

Since Abdal handed me the Cup of Truth
All's equal – mosque and altar are the same.
I burn, surrendering to Gnostic light.
Palace or ruin – both have equal claim.

Thought died, and of me only dust remained.
First I was mud and after fire and flame:
Outside I roasted, inwardly I burned.
Kebab or skewer – both have equal claim.

So passed I by a space that formed no place
And walked before a field which had no name
Perplexed to find creation lacking form.
Exile or homeland – both have equal claim.

My passions led me, greed consumed my soul.
Though reasoning spelt Truth, I sank in shame:
A stone could teach me qualities of love.
Koran or verses – both have equal claim.

Yes, Makhtumkuli lingered at that place
Where sheikhs jumped up to join a dancing game.
The beauty of the One I loved shone forth.
Water or wine — they both have equal claim.

The Burning

In flying close to fire I am aflame,
A moth singed by desire, a lover's game.
I weep. My body is a coal of shame.
I am a ruin – see, grave-robbers came! –
In exile from all men of honoured name.

I freed my mind and made the world stand back.
Look where you tread. Turn into ashes black,
Fly, fly – and burn, whichever way you tack.
Oh, you must read 'ana'I-Hak wa mina 'I-Hak'.
I gulp down wine to try and drown the blame.

Folk don't enjoy me, I don't them enjoy.
Fire burns! I do not any mirth employ:
I wouldn't buy this world for gold alloy.
My friends are enemies who just annoy.
Misunderstood, I stand here scorched and lame.

My mind dwelt in a magic realm of thought
Where soul was in a net of slumber caught;
My body vanished set my heart at nought –

By love and all its magics overwrought.
Thus I became a madman without name.

Here's Makhtumkuli, weeping, out of shape,
Sunk in a mire of thought, without escape.
My inner citadel has suffered rape,
The soul's outside the corpse, sockets agape.
Work lies ahead. Recovery's my aim.

On Growing Old

The more I age, the more my judgement goes.
My age approaches fifty, friends.
And, Lord, my reverence grows less each day
While evil deeds increase against my foes.

From God I am estranged – no hadji I.
Although I sometimes think myself still young
My beard is white, my strength declines, my teeth
Fall out. Alas, my life has passed me by.

Still worldly things are by my heart adored
While lies and gossip occupy my tongue.
The loveliness of women frets my mind.
Stand back, Deceiver! Lust remains my Lord.

Lord God Above, without your gentle aid
How can I free myself? This wretchedness
Snares me within the passions of the flesh
Without the wish to serve you. I'm unmade.

Oh friends, I cry again, I am not whole
Without a faith. It seems my life is mist –

And mist enshrouds the sunlight of my fate.
Shine, Lord, and wake my heavy-sleeping soul!

Lord God, because I am in disarray
Send me a ray of faith bright from beyond.
Forget to count my errors and my sins
Forget, forgive me – prostrate now I pray.

Hell burns as still in flames of lust I stray
Girls guard their purses, men their goods, but I
Stand caught between my fears and palsied hopes.
O Lord, what will befall on Judgement Day?

I Took Up My Pen

I took up my pen and wrote you a letter. Do you not know?
I bewitched a hoopoe and tamed it. Do you not know?
I raised it up to Heaven itself. Do you not know?
Relief came after three days and nights of tears. Do you not know?
I galloped about on an ass, like Jesus. Do you not know?

Do you not know of my days in the desert, weeping like
  Majnun?
I spurted pearls with my tears, 'til like Varqa I died,
Losing all hopes of sweet communion with Gulshah.
How I burned the ever-intensifying heats of love –
Burned, yes burned like Shebli, burned a whole mountain.

Do you not know how, hoopoe-like, I flew from Europe to
  Chin Machin
And saw Belqis in her garden letting down her hair? –
Oh, these were the days of song and stars and Solomon!
My voice was like the nightingale's. The birds that fly
– On Wednesday in the forenoon, this – flew down to hear.

Do you not know that in the cavern Majnun made his magic
With 'Bismillah' first? Entranced, he cried out for his master –

Cried, but God alone heard. Aie, the shrieks of forty lovers
Inspired him with a lust like mountain fire.
Came Thursday, I extinguished it with tears.

Do you not know how Shirvan Khan's banquet amazed us all?
He'll be sent down on Judgement Day if he slips by a hair.
One hundred and twenty lines have thousands of arguments
    in each line.
The thrill of love is deeper than a sleeping river:
My rivers quenched the thirst of forty lovers.

Do you not know my beautiful young hawk, feathers still
    ungrown?
The world in which I slipped was like a muddy ditch.
A lover burns his heart out: earth does not accept.
Pressing whole rocks and mountains through the sieve
I grew a hundred buds even from hostile thorns.

Makhtumkuli says of the Nine Heavens he is the Evening Star,
Brother to the Seven Stars, sibling of Moon and Sun
Dazzler of my sight and apple of my eye,
Spring of Zemzem, the space between Safa and Marwa …
Do you not know, like Solomon, I broke the bounds of Time?

A Lament

Sixty-year-old Sufis (self-declared) –
Small time remains for moons to wax and wane!
In the desert foxes see no hound:
Of hunting sleeping lions they dream again.

'No falcon can compare with me,' says Crow.
To chase one hawk requires a thousand crakes.
The gold-eyed lizard cannot take the sun:
It lurks unseen, waiting to catch small snakes.

Badgers cannot snare the lamest deer,
Nor foxes break a lion cub's defence;
The lizard cannot eat a big snake whole.
You understand? It just needs common sense.

Approaching seventy, they don't repent,
And still love seeing whores cavort and leap.
The infidels all smashed the Kaaba up –
Now Black Yazid sells off its timbers cheap.

Regard the passing time, the turning world,
How poor trudge on beneath the tyrant's load.

They do not give the dervish chance to rest
When travelling along Truth's endless road.

My heart ran out of tolerance. To bear
A grudge at all is evil – that's well-known.
In such surroundings, how my heart grows tired:
I've lost all drive. I must fare on alone.

My enemy is strong, my stars are ill.
O Makhtumkuli says I am a wrecker!
The Kaaba I must see, and hope for Haj.
My mind is set on pilgrimage to Mecca …

Forgive My Sins

O gracious omnipotent Lord –
                    Forgive my sins
O merciful omniscient Lord –
                    Forgive my sins

Should you not reveal your Grace
                    My Will will die within me
Error will overflow its bounds
                    Forgive my sins

My soul of a hundred sorrows
                    Begs your mercy
Gaze down from your great height, O Lord –
                    Forgive my sins

Though I sank in the mire of shame
                    Elevate me from my sins, O far-seeing Lord
With your grace, O all-forgiving One
                    Forgive my sins

Manifest your greatness
                    By laying my heart to rest

By making your favour shine upon me
                Forgive my sins

Thy majesty flees one's imagination
                One can but marvel at Thy diversity
But in response to Thy oneness
                Forgive my sins

Any creature that on earth may dwell
                Who discovers Thy powers of Creation
For the sake of Thy three thousand names
                Forgive my sins

For we are poor *ummah* supplicants
                The *ummah* of Muhammad
Out of respect for the Praised One
                Forgive my sins

Your creation is delectable
                To the palate of the Praised One
For the ransom of Heaven and Earth
                Forgive my sins

For the great gifts of the generous
                For the blood of martyrs
For the life of everything that lives
                Forgive my sins

With reverence to the stars in Heaven
                Reverence to Nawrooz on Earth
Reverence to day and darkest night
                Forgive my sins

For the magnificence of high mountains
                And the lure of landscapes
For the delights of deserts and waters
                Forgive my sins

If there comes no sign from you
                Disaster will descend upon me
Thy Feraghy says, 'O Lord
                Forgive my sins'.

Dawn Is The Time

Friends, be receptive when new days are born!
– When dervish convent doors let in the morn
– When blessings flood them with the pristine light
Of dawn – and Truth sounds clear its hunting horn.

When Sin comes courting, do not let him in.
Deny both sin and self. Thus you will win
Repentance. O, now is the time! Begin!
Now is the time that God forgives all sin.

The Lord will guide you through the narrow pass
Where winds of separation blow, alas!
Be ever ready. When it's time, accept
The wine of friendship from a good man's glass.

Though you might rule this world, so stark in trust,
Come next century you'd be but dust ...
Before the years have fled, fly from your self –
Set up a cabal of the wise and just.

O Makhtumkuli, worlds float in your thought.
When you were young, you only cared for sport:
Now you are thirty and you see more plain;
Those tears that fall announce your sad report.

Crying Crying

I am Jacob, crying cries,
Crying 'Joseph, Joseph',
Crying till blood fills my eyes,
     Crying 'Joseph, Joseph'.

Heavens, weep ye for my ills,
For these ills you cause,
Like Majnun climb I to the hills,
     Crying 'Joseph, Joseph'.

Cloud above the landscape sails
Darkling – yet I cross
Twelve mountains and as many vales
     Crying 'Joseph, Joseph'.

Joseph has fled somewhere unknown;
I weep at lack of news.
So I trudge from town to town
     Crying 'Joseph, Joseph'.

He stumbled down a well, some say.
The moon's less bright than he.

I search Iraq and far away
      Crying 'Joseph, Joseph'.

My pain will Heaven overwhelm;
Birds pining share that pain.
I ruin mountains, Farhad's realm,
      Crying 'Joseph, Joseph'.

Time passes, ever passes by,
My soul burns by the hour.
At dawn and dusk I scan the sky
      Crying 'Joseph, Joseph'.

No lip can Joseph's name withstand –
It's scenting rose on rose.
I seek him out from land to land
      Crying 'Joseph, Joseph'.

O, would my constant tears could hail
Makhtumkuli's friend!
My voice rings like the nightingale
      Crying 'Joseph, Joseph'.

The Pains Of Love

Love caught fire within my heart, and burned and blazed.
Smoke whirling in the wind whipped me like something crazed.
Fate caught me, spinning me upon its wheel.
Who came to see me through the eyes of real desire?
Separation was a storm – both flood and fire.

Swept on, I gained the shores of love, shipwrecked – so null
Real and unreal were hurricanes within my skull.
I fell exhausted, lost in wonderment.
When love unsheathed its dagger, yes, I caught its blade!
Love stripped me naked, left me stranded without shade.

My body held no strength, my corpse no uttering soul
I staggered round, confused and far from whole,
Not weary or alert, alive or dead.
A cloud of sorrow sank to hide my sacrifice,
As destiny's key turned and locked me in its vice.

I had to fight to make grief's spectre disappear:
But Love instructed me and made the problem clear,
Love sorrowed and assisted me to heal.

When beauty bloomed, it brought spring joys of a fresh start.
I have to say all this, dear friends! It broke my heart.

O, hopeful slave to the beloved's charms, whereby
I lost my heart! A songbird of sweet tongues was I –
Encaged! But separation scorched my soul.
Then yearning burned me up, to ash was turned my mind.
And Makhtumkuli's life was tossed upon the wind.

The Twelve Imams

He is the lion, the Prophet's son-in-law.
>For Imam Ali forgive us.

He is my eye's daylight for ever more.
>For Imam Hasan forgive us.

To whom did this false world prove more than true?
On Judgement Day they'll save themselves anew!
Shimr and Yazid tormented these two.
>For Imam Husayn forgive us.

In Nasr-i Sayyar's day it befell
Imams were tortured more than word can tell.
For him thrown down a deep Damascus well
>For Zayn-al-Abidin forgive us.

He is of Fatima Zahra the son:
In truth, he nothing ill has ever done.
His final refuge is Mount Humayun.
>For Muhammad Baqir forgive us.

His wisdom far beyond the heavens towers.
His forefather put on a crown of flowers.
Hajjaj he lived through with three holy powers.
   For Imam Ja'far forgive us.

Who knows what kind of secrets you contain?
O Lord, the answer lies beyond the brain.
You had your friend locked with his foe in pain
   For Imam Musa Kazim forgive us.

I am the worst fool of our caravan,
In love, a mad and wretched sort of man.
A holy place for all in Khorasan.
   For Imam Riza forgive us.

Give me glass for love of Imam's sake.
I'll read the Koran out till voice shall break.
O Lord, for Fatima Qiyam's sake,
   For Muhammad Taqi forgive us.

They suffered countless heartbreaks and dismay.
They'll ride on Buraq on the Judgement Day.
For him who bears the torch upon truth's way,
   For Ali-un-Naqi forgive us.

My heart beats close to yours, our hearts are one.
I will remember you till life is done.
His fame has spread more widely than the sun.
   For Imam Askar forgive us.

If Magog finds his way down Qaf's Mount,
The earth will quail a tyrannous amount.
He will appear here at the Final Count.
   For Sahib-Zaman forgive us.

The poet says, I'm dust beneath the heel.
I'd sacrifice myself to the ideal
For Imams. Wretched am I and I kneel.
        For Abbas Ali forgive us.

When Judgement Day Comes

Brethren become more notorious day by day,
Heresy increases year on year.
Alcohol-drinkers and adulterers, I fear,
Amid the ranks of infamy must stay.

O Muslim brothers, do not deviate!
You'll cross the Sirat Bridge, thin as a hair.
A few more years, Dajjal will come – so they declare –
To stir the world like embers in a grate.

He's dressed in black, his one eye is the keener.
The poor burn in the fire the wicked light –
See where the honest Muslims go when they take flight:
Holy Damascus, Mecca, and Medina.

Jesus and Mahdi bring justice and peace,
But Gog and Magog only tyranny:
They'll dig right through the Qaf Mountains to get at me,
Their knuckles scraping ground, fearsome, obese.

Pen trembles with the pain orphans have born;
The minds of lovers burn with fire and wonder;

The sky will burst and every mountain fall asunder;
Israfil will blow his brazen horn.

Great waters will recede and rivers drain:
Sun, moon, and stars will fail in a relapse
When all the high hills melt and Heaven and Earth collapse.
Only my Lord Himself will then remain.

When Death calls, man will give up all his wealth,
Kin, family, and lastly even breath.
The Lord will then decree the swart Angel of Death,
Even that darkling angel, kill himself!

Save God alone, no living entity
Will then remain. Israfil's horn will die.
In forty days of rain, the seas are earth, earth's sky,
All mingled. Afterwards, new plants will be.

A horse dressed in caparison full brave
Shall come – gold, silver, green and bright scarlet;
Four angels will patrol in unearthly quartet,
Arriving at Muhammad's earthly grave.

An angel's wings will cause the air to shake.
'Yea,' it will say, and when 'Arise!' is said
The grave will open up and soil pour on His head.
Then 'O my *ummah*!', cries he, and will wake.

Fear of that Day of Judgement will prevail
Exceedingly. 'Where are my *ummah*?', cries
He, prostrate – from Sajdah he hesitates to rise
Till guards will come and say, 'Get up, all hail!'

Great Israfil takes up his brazen horn
To stand alert in the Almighty's sight:
Two golden calls he blows anon, to left and right –
And lo! God's creatures, suddenly reborn!

Sneezing, they clamber from that doleful lair,
The grave. Wheezing, they gape up at the sky,
Or queasily survey the changing scene nearby –
For forty days remaining transfixed there.

They see that birds and beasts are all good friends,
That rivers flow together, lip to lip,
That perfect lovers know perfect companionship,
And rise up singing, as the lark ascends!

Demons of Hell hold each a mace of fire –
The scales are set – the sun shines brilliant black –
While those who deal in horses, they are mounted on Buraq –
This one gold-shod, and those in silk attire!

The sun will boil and while the whole world burns
The court's established, judging Wrong from Right.
Brains fry within the skull until they catch alight.
The bread you gave for alms to shadow turns.

Pharaoh, Haman, Shaddad – all infidel –
Will stand there, clutching unbelieving head,
Asking, 'Who revived us from the dismal dead?'
Servants of God will answer them full well.

These infidels will shake in agitation.
As fires rage, their arguments subside:
Now into many ranks of twelve groups they divide.
He comes, thunderous, for their Interrogation.

One group's transformed into a swine brigade,
While other groups transformed to monkeys come,
All chattering. Yet others wander, deaf and dumb.
It's with such suffering that sin's repaid.

Some rush with flames at every orifice,
Some run with pus boiling in throat and lungs,
Mullahs who forsook the Word chew on their tongues.
All this will be, O Lord. It comes to this!

Some moan with liquid fire for a gown,
Some drunken fall in mud and cannot rouse,
Some find grotesque new legs grow spurting from their brows –
So henceforth they must travel upside-down.

This one is pinned beneath an iron mattress
So hot his forehead folds about his nose.
His tongue protrudes into his navel. Comatose,
Past deeds enmesh him snakelike in distress.

Devout chase Infidel from crag to crag.
Snakes large as dromedaries foul the ground.
But Men of God gather in crowds to march around
The world. Muhammad flies his awesome flag!

Prophets face fear and all that it entails:
Sons avoid fathers, fathers shun their sons
In guilt and hate. Muhammad, where the river runs,
Pitches his green flag by the justice scales.

Adam the Prophet murmurs 'O my Son!'
Old Abraham will 'O the One God!' cry.
Moses and Jesus name the Architect on High.
Everyone is fed by everyone.

Prayers from many prophets God beguile;
Both left and right sides self-effacement keep.
So will Muhammad then expose his head and weep,
Repeating 'Oh, my *ummah*,' all the while.

All Men of God to unchecked tears will yield.
They'll not ask of their kin, for good or ill,
From other friends. In due course, golden Israfil
Controls the scales of justice in the field.

All unbelievers have their gowns alight,
To be kicked where the fires of Hell await.
Serpents the size of mules will swiftly infiltrate,
Snakes thick as camels' necks spit flame and bite.

They'll call for help. No one can hear them roar
Although they bray like donkeys crammed in pens.
For nourishment, poisons alone are fed them thence.
They'll serve this sentence out for ever more.

We see what the devout do in their turn:
What work they have and how they fill their hours
So that Muhammad on them all his blessing showers.
Those who do not know this will quickly learn.

Devout folk then will be like paths unwinding,
Some swift as lightning, some as winter's wind,
Some as flood waters, some as hotly-hunted hind,
And some as falcon, wild upon the wing.

This is the Way that takes three thousand years:
Uphill, level, downhill, but always far –
Darker than pitch and sharper than a scimitar.
Yet some will pass through ere a midnight nears.

Others must find their Way by slow parades:
Ten days, perhaps – others, a year in all,
Others fifteen, screaming like kulans in the hall!
Others at last, fifty thousand decades.

His blood is shed, a thousand years unfold:
He crosses Sirat's Bridge at last. Now up
He drinks the precious wine from Kowsar's cup –
This elder now becomes as one year old.

Each youth now wreathes the laurels round his head.
They all have Joseph's beauty, Jesus' age.
They are as David was, as young and just as sage.
Each one embraces now his beloved.

They take their thrones. Their robes are seventy.
Their steeds have reins adorned with malachites.
They enter Paradise, survey its dazzling sights,
Knowing that they will live eternally.

On seventy silk mattresses they'll lie,
The Tuba tree will shade them like a friend,
While seventy silken Houris to their wants attend.
The beauty of the Lord will gratify.

Those who care nothing for the world below,
Drunkards and sluggards – such are Infidels.
'These things will happen', Makhtumkuli here foretells.
Come Judgement Day, all Men of God will know …

The Judgement Of Ali

O men of God, believers, now attend,
And for a tale of miracles prepare.
      This happened when beloved Ali
Was in the mosque, his mind consumed by prayer.

He knelt with reverence, transfixed against
The altar, with his gaze upon the Book.
      Of his companions, young and old,
None were without reflection in their look,

When through an archway flew a ring-necked dove.
Ali saw it. When its flight was done,
      It settled by him. Lo, it spoke:
'Salaam aleykum, Ali, Bravest One.'

In clearest voice, the supernatural bird
Declared, 'You're all that's said or sung
      Of faith and holiness. I've flown
From distant fields, wherein I have five young.

'To feed my flightless brood I flit from earth
To heaven's height and all that lies between.

I am as much a child of God
As countrysides where I seek food are green.

'O Bravest One, my search led everywhere
And gratitude to God flew in my breast.
            Singing, I garnered up the grains
So needful for my young within the nest.

'I never thought of enemies, not I!
Carefree was I, except the care I own
            For those I nourish. Suddenly –
The shadow of a foe flashed o'er the sown.

'A falcon swift and speckled soared above –
Free as air and fast as breeze. From high
            It plunged the moment that I looked.
Could I fly half as fast, Ali? Not I!

'Yet driven by the fear that powers a wing
I cut the air, the wind itself I shaved:
            And now upon your threshold, pray
Your mercy, Ali, Brave One, to be saved.'

To all of nature Ali was friend
Who, listening gravely to this tale of flight,
            Beckoned the bird with gentle hand.
'Poor feathered thing, I'll shield you in your plight.'

Cooing, the dove came forward, ruffled still
With fear, and sought refuge in Ali's sleeve.
            It did so. Next, the falcon came,
Bright-winged, and calling, 'Ali, by your leave,

'Hark to my tale as well,' and with salaams
It added, 'Then decide.' In Ali's face
        The bird dared look with hooded eye;
Forthwith before its judge it put its case:

'My territory covers arid plain,
Mountains and scree wherein no rivers run.
        Here must I seek such morsels as
I can. Your dove? Mere meat to me, Brave One!

'Feather and bone am I, my craw untouched
By food these three days past. I'm not divine,
        Just flesh, as God decreed. I starve!
Give me the dove Law designates as mine.'

He flattered Ali then, addressing him
As Wielder of the great Sword Zulfiqar,
        The King who broke Duldul the Horse.
But Ali rose to call his slave Kanbar.

Kanbar abased himself and begged to serve
The Brave One whom – he said – all must revere.
        With sternness, Ali ordered thus:
'Go then, and bring my jewelled dagger here.'

The falcon now with apprehensive voice
Asks Ali what he means to do. 'Abide
        My will, O bird. Touch not this dove.
Instead you'll eat of meat sliced from my side.'

The dagger came, and straightaway was unsheathed,
Its blade agleam like sunlight, bright and fresh.
        As Ali made to plunge it down,
The falcon cried, 'Don't mar your holy flesh!',

And with his talons seized the lifted arm.
'For those Unborn who dream of being made –
     And for the Blessed – the hope lies in
Your sacred hand. Pray drop this murder blade!'

The falcon ceased then in his birdlike shape
And stood transformed. Cried he, 'Ali, the Blessed,
     I am no bird – nor is this dove.
Our aim's fulfilled, and you have passed the test.'

Courage, compassion: these were not in doubt.
They stood before the King, and by-and-by
     Took wing like angels, feathered bright,
High to the hectares of unmeasured sky.

It matters not what form the Spirit takes –
Be sure to load with alms a beggar's bowl:
     The scent of Kindness pleases God.
Forgiveness is the essence of the Soul.

So ends this verse and, like an ancient scroll,
Is furled. If words may elevate the world
     Then Makhtumkuli is a star
With Master Ali in the sun's dance whirled.

Birds Of The Air

Meditating on all things afresh,
I heard my soul cry 'God' –
That soul, when free in wisdom, wisely clothed
In blood and nerve and evanescent flesh.

Perchance you do not find the path traversed,
Perchance you do not know,
Perchance you cannot seek the way to God:
You'll find yourself in sorrow deep immersed.

Observe the palms that grow so bounteously.
You see the rose that blooms,
You see the grass. O blind man, also see
All are part of one great Unity!

Temptation urges pleasure. Oh, to sport
Freely with women fair!
To feast and drink – enjoyment without mind!
To sleep within some lofty palace court!

My heart, you're little but a market-stall,
With pride bartered for love.

Too cheap! Every affair's an auction sale:
You cry aloud your wish to have it all.

Unpreened, the wings of birds are opening,
Pages of books spread wide.
Yon flocks of pigeons rise with murmurous call,
Flying, yet starving, starving on the wing …

Nightingale says, 'I guard bowers,
Awaiting blessed spring.
My love is for a rose-bed
In a garden full of flowers.'

Lover says, 'Illallah', yes!
Swallow says, 'Hamdu lillah'.
Stork says, 'Kul huwallah',
With open heart and tenderness.

Bat calls out, 'O Lord', in flight,
'You led me to this path,
So save me from the moon,
The sun, the wind. Hide me in night!'

Phoenix cries, 'I'm passenger!'
Hoopoe says, 'Here in
This world of falsity
For Solomon I'm messenger.'

Bustard is in a state of shock.
Flying round surprised
By life he wheels about
In time and circles like a clock.

Crane proclaims he flies with care.
'I drink of Baghdad's pools,
Winter in Hindustan,
And nest among the tulips there.'

Owl says, 'My problem's one of thought.
I have beads and I pray.
Ruins provide a home
For me, by pain always distraught'.

The horned owl says, 'I'm poor and stark,
A servant merely, I,
Who calls the Lord's name loud
Repeatedly into the dark'.

The sparrow says, 'I know I flitter
Here and there, flying
Between these three small trees,
To lay my eggs in such a twitter'.

The peregrine says, 'In a spell
Of drink and ecstasy
I quite forgot my God
Within my darkened prison cell'.

Francolin is full of praise.
Duck is hard at prayer.
And while the goose honks loud
Its eye seeks out the sea always.

Canaries sing in calm or wind.
Peacock pursues its whims –
Peacock with many hymns
Flies to the ravaged heart of Ind.

Wails from the parrot's painted face
Come as it waits for death.
Speaking the tongue of man
It mingles with the populace.

The fallow deer says that she's wailing.
'I am true to you.
But for my precious young
Who suffer pain my heart is failing'.

Wolf says, 'Mine are the splendid chases.
I gain a livelihood
Wherever I may run
In stony desert or oases.'

Seven earths are built, so vain
That everyone sings praise.
Grasses say, 'Rabbana'
Shining in the Nawruz rain.

On Judgement Day, the day when each is
Judged, you will be told
'Give up your evil ways',
Just as the Holy Koran teaches.

As Joseph was, hopeful remain,
As Job was, patient be,
If you're suffering
As Jacob was in Canaan's plain.

Hark, my soul's ecstatic sound!
My passion says 'Rejoice!' –
Your generosity
Won't fail when Judgement Day comes round.

O Makhtumkuli, look at me
And let your tear drops flow,
Nor blame me when I talked
Among my loved ones, privily.

Exhortation In Time Of Trouble

My fortune seems to be taking wing.
Since we pray and rend our clothes
Fulfil our wishes, O Great Lord.
The Kyzylbash have ruined everything.

Send warriors to the steppes, where habitable,
Make our homeland structures robust,
Cool the heads of our brave youth.
Above all, let our food all be served on one table.

Let dervishes pray without unseemly interference
And the young as formerly gather for the dance.
May all our peoples enjoy the spring of their lives,
And difficult winter days have disappearance.

If Turkmens would only tighten the Belt of Determination
They could drink the Red Sea in their strength.
So let the tribes of Teke, Yomut, Gokleng, Yazir, and Alili
Unite into one proud nation.

What is Soul? Makhtumkuli tries to understand it.
Let us not be subjugated by the Kyzylbash!
Grant us a union of Teke and Yomut
And let Kemal Khan command it.

Be Not Poor!

O Ummah of Muhammad, be not poor,
Or else your kith and kin will leave your door
As strangers. Brothers too will lose respect.
Your foes will laugh and vex your friends the more.

A poor man goes barefoot, showing his need.
At meetings they will seat him low indeed,
While if he rides a horse it's called an ass –
A rich man's ass, of course, is called a steed!

Just ask a favour, then see what you get!
Ask friends for loans – you'll just remain in debt.
At councils, what you say will not be heard;
You might as well catch water with a net.

Wrestling is honest sport, fighting is rash.
One who degrades another is mere trash;
Gossip about the Holy is unwise –
A gossip's breath turns all to fire and ash.

This poet praises God for everything!
Death calls alike on beggar and on king.
A hasty youth will find his troubles mount,
While patient men with growing joy will sing.

Makhtumkuli's Advice

Never speak sharply to a fellow man.
The poor are aided by your courtesy.
Stay distant from the sinner if you can.
Doing your work well needs efficiency.

When meeting orphans, greet them with a smile
And, better yet, provide a meal meanwhile.
Comfort the sad in gently hopeful style.
Support the helpless man with constancy.

Though poverty brings pain with it, perforce,
It does not kill. So smile – a dog or horse
Conceals its weakness from a wolf. Of course
Such wiles are needed 'gainst the enemy.

With brave men, what is promised is then done.
Don't argue when there's no case to be won.
And modesty becomes us, everyone,
As justice does a Sultan's sovereignty.

The fields grow green, with flowers ever young.
O Makhtumkuli thanks God for his tongue,
As advocates plead cases yet unsung.
There's elegance shown in a bended knee.

Visions And Fantasies

Dainty different dishes set before you –
But with no salt no savour to the bread.
No savour to a future still unknown,
No eyes ahead and no eyes in the head.

Legs are for walking, hands for holding hands –
The faithful lift their hands to God when young
In thanks for health. With practice, ears can hear
Though not a word is spoken by the tongue.

God fashioned souls from something like dried mud.
Faith flowers from souls as roses from fine mould.
The bud knows not the flower, nor flower the seed:
We know the One, though He remains untold.

The happy man will find his means enough,
The preacher always finds the means to preach.
But tongue and heart stand still until we find
In every heart, love speaking each to each.

Our acts of shame will still proliferate
Unless the end is one that God decides:

While worldly talk is bread without its salt
Unless it dwells on subjects such as brides.

Close your eyes and grit your teeth. You may,
In May, remember winter winds impend.
Rely on God – your deeds are his Design:
Be patient! All will end up in the end!

O Makhtumkuli struggles in a net
Of fantasy, and does not understand.
My visions speak. Friends, do not blame me for
My words – grander come only from the grand.

Till Judgement Morn

We worship our Creator when we're newly born,
To think of him again perhaps – only when trouble-worn!
This is what Makhtumkuli says at russet dawn
As the night steals off with its single silver horn,
When he thinks on the blacknesses of Judgement Morn!

Be grateful for your health before you meet disease,
Honour your illnesses before you die,
Appreciate dry land before you drown at sea.
Be happy for your youth before your years drain by.
In every case there stands the matter of degree.

As to your inner self: have you control of it?
You let your tongue prefer its sound to better sense,
You let your eyes devour a girl and flatter her –
Meanwhile, your pride grows like a tree, shady, immense.
Before you knew your own sly ways, happy you were!

Once you were grown adult, action was all your joy –
To chase a hare or deer, or wrestle with a friend,
Even by sword to take a country or a town,

As if your roving days on earth would never end,
And you were just a verb – a verb and not a noun.

But such events can never stay the changing world.
Leave boastfulness and give your favourite gifts away.
This is what Makhtumkuli says at russet dawn,
'Through brief, make yours a day of light, till light of day
Fades before the blacknesses of Judgement Morn!'

Unholiness

Seas are covered, mountains fallen,
Orphans shedding tears.
Lords who are the sons of whores
Spread their sins like pollen.

The call to prayer can scarcely stir a martyr.
The studies of the mullahs are in vain.
Now tea and 'nas' are all the Kazis know.
Corruption shows, with all its foul stigmata.

Respect for answered prayers is in a poor way.
Those who would pass as Sufis scream and, more,
Claiming to be awlias, leap about ...
Ishans are to be found in every doorway.

Young girls parade in attitudes of boredom,
Their painted faces covered by black veils.
They now commence to decorate themselves
With coins they earn from evil acts of whoredom.

Riches are all that money-lenders savour.
The wealthy man of *zekat* takes no heed.

Repent! What evils have I seen, as friend
Is wounding friend and neighbour wounding neighbour!

O Makhtumkuli, mullahs without merit
Rush turbaned through the land like savage wolves.
Still ravening, they hunt our honour down,
Devouring everything we should inherit.

An Age Without Morality

This is the age of dead morality:
Wrong-doers from the decent turn and flee;
Once more the base, despising noble blood,
Insinuate, and ape, nobility.

Their prayers no longer bother to beseech
Their God, now that mullahs no long preach.
Even the Kazi, long the Prophet's voice –
The Kazi holds his hand out for *bakhshish*.

Sultans now laugh at justice in eclipse.
These derelictions spell apocalypse,
When farthings buy a mufti's best decree,
And tyrants die with no prayer on their lips.

The poor are pallid, starving, and distraught,
While bulging bellies mark another sort –
Those vile oppressors beating the oppressed,
Whose whippings form a bloody kind of sport.

Nobody listens when a scholar sings.
To the Creator no one tribute brings.

67

Sufis no longer read the Holy Book,
Forswear religion for more worldly things.

Too many Sufis are that but in name,
Eating the food of tyrants without shame,
Hoping Lord So-and-So will call them good,
Haunting the scented thresholds of ill-fame.

Young people, once so fair, are now turned grey,
Backs turn to humps and hands to feet of clay.
Brothers meanwhile pile baggage on their heads,
Shuffling along towards the Judgement Day.

A wise man, feeling heart and senses smother,
Seeks remedies for all the pained world's bother.
Declaring sin has sullied everything,
He thinks to slip from this world to another.

Now is the day of dissipated lords.
The tongues of gossips wag like those of bawds.
So who remains to seek a finer goal
When love itself grows dim, without rewards?

This sugared Kazi speaks with double tongue,
No longer spending nights his books among,
Or following the right path for *shariah*.
The world of faith he trades for passion's dung.

Says Makhtumkuli, 'Find your path and learn
God gives you only five days to discern
The truth. Where are the souls already fled?
Each one of us must follow in our turn.'

A Topsy-Turvy Time

I have a quarrel with my land and age.
No one can tell blessing and advantage
From handicap and wretched tyranny.
What Islam means puzzles even the sage.

No one speaks truth or wisdom any more.
No one distinguishes lies from the law.
No one can tell what's dirty from what's clean.
The line 'twixt fair and foul we now ignore.

Our people have no chuckles and no charms.
The rich no longer grant the poor their alms.
Mothers are shameless and their daughters flirt.
Manners are lost amid all such alarms.

On others' property men keep an eye:
Their hearts are full of spite, their ways are sly.
Justice is dead, so murder stalks the street.
Compassion? Love? All that has long gone by.

O Makhtumkuli, does your soul not dwell
Here but a little time? And in that spell
The soul must soar above this tawdry age.
What good or bad is, no one's soul can tell.

The Hill Outside Our Village

The hill outside our village looks
Much like a horse's saddle. We'll
See useless people who are like
    Bad scripts which in gold leaf congeal.

This world is deep, enduring deep!
You might drown in it – do not sleep,
Rein in your pride! Better to weep –
    Life is the maze through which we steal.

Those without wives have tears to spare;
Those without children no jewels wear,
And without brothers nothing dare:
    Their happy days hold wan appeal.

The wicked leave no permanent
Bequest, while nobles rest content.
But worldly riches? – Quickly spent:
    Only a son's your lasting weal.

Upon a wound, salt is no *kaif*
To soothe the bitterness of life.

A decent husband's naughty wife
     Is like a wound that will not heal.

She sleeps with snakes, her neck around,
Or cuddles with some mangy hound.
But when a virtuous wife is found –
     She is a jewel, a man's ideal.

O Makhtumkuli, some, I've heard,
Are happy. Sadness is preferred.
He who won't accept my word
     Is but a ship without a keel.

What To Appreciate

A miller would mistreat a hawk, it stands
To reason, since he knows not what it's for.
If diamonds fall into a shepherd's hands
He'll use them all for flints. Could he care more?

Who will not drink God's verse will dry remain;
Who cannot drink God's word will worms sustain;
Who pines for love like Majnun goes insane –
Should Leyla's beauty find a shuttered door?

Who keeps tight fists will never be a lord;
Who has not worked has never rest adored;
Who has not been by hunger's spasms gnawed –
For him a fresh-baked loaf has how much draw?

Riches are valued only when they're lost,
And when they're spent, you just can't count the cost.
He who has not in raging fever tossed –
How can he prize the healthy years in store?

He who does not drop anchor deep enough
Will find his ship drifts with the winds that puff.

Whose boat has never sunk in storm waves rough –
Will he appreciate the stable shore?

No coward holds the moral ground, alas!
Till tired, no-one values the patient ass.
The swan that's never seen a desert's mass –
Will she prize placid lakes where reed-beds snore?

Who has not fled to exile from a foe,
Who was not bruised by separation's blow,
Who has not pined for all to love and know –
Who values peace who never sampled war?

The poet says, 'Here's how this matter ends:
Be thankful for the present moment, friends.'
He who cannot see where my wisdom tends –
How could he prize a thousand verses more?!

Perfection

High mountains, do not boast about your height
For you'll become as flat as molten gold.
Rough seas, do not be proud about your might,
For you'll become in time land dry and old.

The forest lion and elephant, meanwhile,
Shrink mouse-like when mosquitoes sting and poke:
The mighty crocodile who rules Oxus and Nile
Counts for no more than badly beaten moke!

My talk of Judgement Day is not a joke:
Unfair beating's a crime you'll one day cry on.
Oppressors then will have to play the moke –
The poor, of course, will be the forest lion.

Riders prance by – we see them cheek-to-cheek
With lovely women – antics Heaven mocks.
Such faithless poseurs really are the weak.
With faith, you pass Above strong as an ox.

With everyone, you try to put them right.
Why don't you keep your own advice in mind?

Follow the wise – you might regain your sight.
Follow the daft – you might as well be blind.

If, like Lukman, you have a panacea,
Like Alexander, conquer land and sea,
Like Rustam, rule those tribes both far and near:
You'd be a giant – with humility.

Humility! says Makhtumkuli. Hush!
Follow perfection, love the straight and tall,
Work like the patient ox, sing like the thrush.
Listen! Perfection is the end of all.

Loss

Suppose a partridge loses chicks, can she
Do less than mourn her babes where they belong?
Suppose a nightingale should lose its red
Tulip, can it but sing its yearning song?

If a jenny loses her young foal
What will she do but search for it, alone?
And equally, if camels lose their young,
What can they do but roll about and moan?

And this gazelle – if she loses her fawn
And strains to hear its feeble bleat again,
Does she not crouch, as sorrow mists her eyes,
And weep once more, poor thing? Is that not pain?

Suppose you kick a lame man's crutches off –
Is he not bound to suffer hopelessly?
A sow confronted by a larger foe
Defends her litter quite ferociously.

How can we bear the pangs of final partings,
Though Death may steal upon us while we sleep?
Even if Makhtumkuli's son were nothing but
A cub, what then? What should he do all day but weep?

Pity My Helplessness

O friends, pity my helplessness
Before a cruel destiny.
My soul is wounded to its core –
My own dear child was ripped from me.

My time of happiness has flown,
All tarnished is my golden throne,
Chill autumn wind has overthrown
My tender growing sapling tree.

Untimely death, allowing no appeal,
Has cast me down the well of pain I feel.
My heart is shattered quite on fortune's wheel –
My feeble body is a falling tree.

I cannot rest a moment, cannot stay –
Not in this world of imminent decay:
I'm blind to everything except dismay,
Which can but leave me weeping helplessly.

Like moths aflame whichever way they dart
Fly sorrows to the candle of my heart.

My back is bowed, my eyes drip tears that smart
To quench this anguish from fate's cruelty.

Alas, how deeply sorrows burn!
I scream aloud, I scream and yearn
To hold my son close. His return
Alone might salve my beggary.

So Makhtumkuli can't abate
His cries, such is his inner state.
His loss has left him desolate
And black is all futurity.

My Father

In the Year of the Fish, Death came on Nawruz Day,
To block my father's path in stark array.
Papa was sixty-five then. So fate rules
Our world. Death struck – and took his breath away.

He played no part in man's grubbing for gold.
From mundane pleasures he'd himself withhold.
Old ragged clothes were all he ever wore.
The Afterlife was what he'd fain behold.

He said, Earth shall decay and life will end,
Peace quits the day, sleep does not night attend.
Agnostics doubt: Faithful alone are free.
Friends of my father are the Prophet's friend.

What I saw I would not merely guess.
He is a holy refuge God will bless.
Angels and demon-things will play their part,
Yet father's tomb will not go sentryless.

I met Three Hundred Leaders, wise and white,
And saw my father reached the Forty's height.

Among the nobles, he was of the Seven,
And passes now among the Abdals bright.

Though men must die, his name still echoes round.
This secret, people know, does not resound.
His home is Paradise, his soul shines there:
His body lies contented under ground.

O Makhtumkuli, keep your secrets nice!
So find and serve a good man without price.
All who are true friends of my grand Papa
On Judgement Day will enter Paradise.

Abdulla Absent

Abdulla left home in a holy throng.
All who leave return – but these forgot.
Muhammad Safa also went along.
Well-wishers waved, returned: the pilgrims not.

Most children sleep close by their father's bed.
O Lord, have they been seen by close kindred?
The moon has waxed and waned as years have fled.
Months and years return: the pilgrims not.

Those who taste poison may quite soon get well.
Shepherds get paid and then go home to dwell.
People who go on Hajj a six months' spell
Return Hajis at last: the pilgrims not.

Say, those who *caravanserai* have made,
Have any heard why Abdul was delayed?
Why, those who went to India to trade,
Even they came back: the pilgrims not.

The rain came pouring down, a thing distraught.
Wayfarers were destroyed with homes they sought

While in the road a girl stood over-wrought
To see the pilgrims come: but they did not.

Does not the heart of him who falls soon rise?
Who leaves returns; who laughs has weeping eyes.
Could passers-by not answer your surmise?
Unknowns have all returned; the pilgrims not.

Now sleep fails Makhtumkuli, pained and vexed,
Not knowing where to seek his old friends next.
The earth itself seems equally perplexed.
All ask Where are they? Answer pilgrims not.

Making My Dear Life Lost

Making my dear life lost to all that's good,
An evil fate wrought awesome sacrilege,
Hurling the books I'd written to the flood,
To leave me bookless with my grief and rage.

The foe surrounded us. Surprised, we shook
And scattered – so we all our friends forsook.
As for my five years' work, my precious book,
The Kyzylbash destroyed it, page by page.

Then some were left behind, tired and afraid,
And some of us were into slavery made,
Freedom to gain if ransom then was paid –
The price according to each captive's gauge.

This fate has dragged me almost to the ground.
My being wept with sorrow so profound
To see my manuscript untimely drowned
That rivers all were hateful at this stage.

Many's the man who meets with some success,
While many more are starving, more or less.

The world echoes to all their loud distress.
My own lament was heard throughout an age.

We stagger under fate's too harsh duress:
It proffers well but lies, to our distress.
So Makhtumkuli speaks the truth out. Yes,
There's nothing can my broken heart assuage.

Defy The Fiend!

O man of God, from evil shrink, because
The Day of Judgement soon will come. Beware
The lure of gold that gleams in Satan's jaws.
Such lures bring shame on you beyond repair.

Your lust shouts, 'Do it! Seize it for relief!'
But conscience whispers, 'No – God sees a thief'
Though you are blind, He watches you with grief:
Forget your impulse, let shame keep its lair.

One way lies Sin, the other lies reward.
On Judgement Day you'll answer to the Lord:
Pure acts mean well – unclean are not ignored,
No doubt. Of this you'd better be aware.

The sweet spring of your life hour by hour,
So let prayer in this fertile season flower:
Virtues bear fruit – which crime can soon devour:
Restrain your soul, let virtues flourish there.

Raise not your head on high, or storm defy,
And tremble not, the slightest urge deny.

The hearing of your ears on God rely,
The speeches of your lips of God declare.

Say, lowly traveller, with your tent unfurled,
How long will you among the Quick be hurled?
When you, for fair or ill, pass from this world,
The next will bring your Judgement, ill or fair.

When Satan says, 'It's sweet – forget your soul!',
God says, 'Defy the Fiend, stay in control!'
So Makhtumkuli, seize the blazing coal:
Then go and do it – if pain you can bear!

Love's Torments

Rivers of love surged forth and overflowed.
I surfaced with a cloudburst in my blood –
The throne of heart o'erturned – the world in code –
I swam and swam, a candle in the flood!

Sleeping I dreamed and waking I arose.
Love's cruel – so I have read, I think –
Its fatal dram of ecstasy I chose:
I seized the chalice. Now I have to drink!

Dark gales from my beloved blew. Eclipse
Brought separation. Hope was overdue.
She held her hand out but withdrew her lips,
And I lay drowning in a fevered brew.

To that bewitching eye and brow I came.
The fires of love, once lit, were blazing grass.
I started to engrave the sacred name
Of my beloved on my inmost glass.

These mirrors that we build within the mind
Betray us and our love's image misplace.

I long to read her countenance, but find.
I'm gazing at my own love-clouded face!

From this reflection once I journeyed far
Beyond, I hoped, passion's deceitful scope.
I met the thief of love in that bazaar;
At once, the glass was shattered – and all hope!

I quaffed the hemlock offered by my friend.
If poison's remedy, trust is its price.
From slave to wrecker next I did descend –
Wrecking my self, love's inbuilt edifice.

Whoever ventures in that stormy realm,
Says Makhtumkuli, finds there's no escape
Or cure, my friends, from pains that overwhelm
The wanderer in dooms of female shape!

The Only End Of Love

O, my beloved! – Who could tell her my desire?
I'm like an ember in the furnace of love's heat
When only my beloved's kiss can quench the fire –
Not any lashing storm of rain or snow or sleet.

The Wanderer passed on, leaving an empty shell.
The Coward broke the bond a Hero forged so well.
And my Beloved made my life a living hell,
Its agony well seasoned for this Fool to eat.

I've lost her somewhere now, beyond the tell of touch.
My fortune sleeps, my fortune slumbers all too much.
Peace dies of hurt. My heart within its little hutch
Beats on until I see her comeliness complete.

My pain constricts me with the coils of a snake.
Jesus would not know, or Lukman, what to take
To loose these toils. My head, my vision is opaque.
Only by speaking out I ease this raging gleet.

You piled up all these earthly goods – and then you laughed!
To gain one cent you made a thousand sweat and graft.

If world is river, you make but a fragile craft.
How long can you continue strolling Easy Street?

Whoever took a single penny from this life?
It ends in ruin: grief and care are always rife.
O son of human seed, here is the end of strife:
You finish up with ash and dust your last retreat.

Where, Makhtumkuli, is the country you call home?
You labour greatly but who owns this land you roam
Where fate prevails? You'll earn a stretch of loam,
God willing, wrapped up in six yards of winding sheet …

The Nightingale

I'm a nightingale. Here's my sad song
From my Garden of roses. Now I've begun.
See the tears in my eyes? There they belong.
What pleasure in life when loving is done?

Kohl becomes my lover's eyes,
Darker than the evening skies,
Lips as sweet as butterflies,
Warm the jungles of her hair.

Alas, my soul in frailty
Takes comfort in her cruelty –
Even her eyebrows chasten me!
So how endure that maiden's stare?

And yet in grieving I rejoice –
Her raven hair allows no choice.
My songbird of the tuneful voice
Makes madrigals of parting fair.

Why does my heart neglect its duties?
Because she is the Khan of beauties

And as my orchard where the fruit is
Perfumes gardens everywhere.

She lives where towers with sunrise flame.
Her promise was – *but mine's the blame* ...
Mengli's the music that's her name –
Yet there's an end to our affair.

I'm a nightingale. This is my song
For her I love, who dwells among
Bowers where I may no more belong.
Now Makhtumkuli's heart's laid bare.

Marrying

If you're ambitious to sour your youth
And by age be harried –
Or if you yearn for a snowy white beard –
Go and get married!

Oh yes, it's great to be venerable.
To your grave you'll be carried.
And if you wish manhood's roses to fade,
Go and get married!

All men ever need is a bed – but kids
From trouble are quarried.
If you aspire to become an old ass,
Go and get married!

Although flirtation may suit you just fine,
By pain you'll be parried.
Still if you're needing that kind of scene,
Go and get married!

You might well be feeling as high as a kite
But spring hasn't tarried.

To hasten the autumn with all of its pains,
Go and get married!

When you set out first you really don't know
How much you'll be worried.
To taste all the good and bad of the earth,
Go and get married!

O Makhtumkuli, you feared not this world.
Your travels were varied.
If you're wishing to follow the Prophet's true path –
Go and get married.

Two Wives

Poor wretched man who keeps two wives! His plight
Entails an endless squabble, day and night.
Each wife has grievances as dogs have fleas,
Which he can never ever settle quite.

And if there's one he loves and one he'd shun,
He'll be shown up. He must not favour one
Or he'll end up frustrated and ignored.
Ignoring them, he'll prove a figure of fun.

One day she'll be a song bird, sweet and meek,
Charming both friends and strangers for a week.
Next week, she'll stamp and throw ashes about
And, when she sees her husband, will not speak.

If he can't coax her out of all such games
Or call the pair of them by pretty names –
Well, dolts like that are scarcely proper men!
So wives plus husband rightly make – three dames!

O Makhtumkuli, let's not that way sink!
Better wed once with understanding. Link
Your life to one. Lord, save us from bad girls,
Or else I'll think – oh, who knows what I'll think …

When The Sun Drives Its Daggers

When the sun drives its daggers in the earth
You are the moon who will eclipse it.
You are the Creator's filigree
The finest tensioned bow of Isfahan.

The fibres of your hair are silver thread –
Snares, so no man can pass you by.
Your mouth is a well-spring of life's waters
April can only blush before your smile.

You are the ruby of the sunset rose.
In India you are sugar, honey in Bulgaria.
You are the freshest flower by Oxus banks
Zuleika, Joseph's loved one, is your peer.

Whoever is the strongest is called Sage:
They ease the pain of every Man of God.
They say that 'Jackals eat the finest melons'.
The man who keeps you is too fortunate.

Your fame extends beyond the mountains of Cathay
Those who meet you marvel at your beauty.

You are the rose-red crystal prized in Hindustan
Golconda's decorated reed made flesh.

When Makhtumkuli hides his heart from you
Perhaps you hear the sound of grinding teeth.
Supposing the Creator fancies you –
Perhaps he'll match you with a poorer man.

Everything Openly

When Nawruz falls the world takes colour – openly:
Clouds cry aloud, mountains gather haze – openly:
Even the lifeless come to life – breathing openly:
Plants, before unseen, grow up and blossom – openly:
All creatures benefit or do us harm – openly:
They breed their kind and stealthily go by – openly:
Birds open beaks and sing when summer comes – openly.

Safe in his sandy home the crab opens his watery site,
Earth fills with grasses soft, to gratify our sight.
Each living thing revives as if with wine alight –
A thousand songs the nightingale sings from its height
And every tissue marvels at the songster's flight.
With tulips laden bows the land for our delight:
The whole world is on show now, shouting openly.

With dance and music merry does the earth's face glow;
Tune after tune, the *dutah* plies unwearied bow.
To loving souls, God's words eternal life bestow,
To loveless souls, Mortality its kiss will blow.
These weeks of spring pile green and greener green on show.

Here Resurrection trips with Judgement on her brow –
The world's great courtroom welcomes new souls openly.

Don't worship luxury, wealth's stuff will not remain
And woes are all a spendthrift's house can entertain.
Avoid what's written in fate's scroll? The hope is vain!
Don't harness up your soul with false regrets in train;
Good deeds are good when planned – but twice as good again
When practised. Time rolls on while men their sleep obtain.
When deeds are evil, ah!, hellfire's your gain, openly.

This poet weeps! Fortune presents an empty bowl:
Coarse hands, bare feet, bear witness to a famished soul.
Wishes are false when life slips from the heart's control.
My soul burns in my body like a flaming coal,
My hands stretch trembling out to God for mercy's dole.
Servant am I, but trust my Lord to make me whole
On Judgement Day, wear mercy like a rose – openly.

When I Cease To Be

Round this world, rich and arid,
Let's look. What will surveys reveal?
The towers built a goodly deal
By Alexander and Jamshid.

Lions and tigers haunt the wild
In forests luminous and green.
Dew-damp meadows next are seen,
Creeks and springs with water mild.

From nothing did the Lord create.
Mountains are the lords of earth:
Ask them, they'll talk of Noah's birth!
About them prayers congregate.

Rejoice, untruthful world, rejoice!
Both gay and sad men fade away:
Soon only lofty hills will stay
With snow drifts blocking sight and voice.

Cloud round their peaks will not disperse
Or dissipate their upward thrust.

Nor shall Time grind them into dust
Or frost disrupt their groves diverse.

No single hamlet will remain:
Only gardens to behold
Where virgins once had sweetly strolled
And nightingales trilled their refrain.

Whoever lives will soon in graves have lain;
Says Makhtumkuli, death devours all sins.
The sky remains, while earth in orbit spins.
The sun will rise and set, moon wax and wane …

Versifier's Note

Seeking to place the distinguished poet Makhtumkuli in some kind of equivalent English context, I see a shadowy likeness.

Makhtumkuli discarded the elaborate and stilted language of Chagatay for a more direct manner of speech. It is this that renders his poems living things, still sung today. In the same period in England, the chief poet of the Augustan age was Alexander Pope, whose poetry delights in literary artifice. Towards the end of the century, William Cowper rejects Augustan elaboration, to write more simply of country walks and such matters.

Beyond that, parallels fall down. Makhtumkuli, a practitioner of the *rub'ai* form, delights in rhyme at least as greatly as Pope, and cleaves mainly to the end-stopped rhyme. He is the great moralist. For him, the world often seems less substantial than the world to come.

> My mind dwelt in a magic realm of thought
> Where soul was in a net of slumber caught

He is the poet of distress, not of despair, and as such is well-suited to be the poet-hero of the new nation of Turkmenistan, which has many problems to overcome, spiritual ones not least.

My qualifications as versifier of a Central Asian poet are alarmingly few, I must admit. As a visitor to many Islamic countries and a reader of the Koran, I am not entirely a stranger to the Muslim world. But with the tone of many of these poems I am completely familiar: for I was brought up in a strict Non-Conformist faith which was as much concerned with Judgement Day as any follower of the Prophet. The reckoning to come was a diurnal concern.

When I began my task, it was as a dilettante. My first poem I versified in Ashkhabad in May 1994. It was achieved in much the same spirit as the one in which one tackles a difficult crossword – to see if it can be done.

This attitude rapidly changed, developing into a genuine love of the self-imposed task. It would have been impossible, of course, without Dr Azemoun's translations and encouragement. I found myself becoming more and more deeply preoccupied – not with the task as such but with the processes of Makhtumkuli's thought.

The visionary nature of the poem we present here as 'The Revelation' was influential in bringing me closer to the remarkable man who wrote it.

So I became a gale! – And to the tall
Blue vault of heaven and the deepest pall
Of earth did blow!

Here is a man preoccupied with the possibility of transcendence for a humankind whose circumstances are in general adverse.

To say a word about translation/versification. Chinese poetry is concrete in form and has been translated into English with some success – by Arthur Waley, Ezra Pound, and A.C Graham, among others. I know of no models for translating from Turkic. Of course, there is the *Rubai'yat of Omar Khayyam*, whose elegant despairs are seductive. I have tried to avoid Fitzgerald's 'orientalising': no easy task when one has loved the poem since childhood.

Fidelity to the sentiment of the original is impossible without a regard for the verse forms in which they were embodied. After all, poems are – to be successful – patterns of sound. I have sometimes thought it expedient to depart from what English readers might regard as a surfeit of rhyme; and for reasons of diversity, needful when the poems are gathered together in one volume, I have occasionally embraced other metres, other rhyme-schemes.

One element of the original I have retained only reluctantly. Makhtumkuli has a habit of concluding a poem employing his own name, even apostrophising himself. Dr Azemoun explains the reason for this trope in his Introduction. However, the practice is alien in English prosody; Wordsworth and others do not address themselves.

And enterprises of great pith and moment,
Says William Shakespeare, often go awry.

It will not do. Yet one must be faithful to, and have faith in, the original. Possibly the question is, Is one writing for the audience in Ashkhabad or London? If so, then the answer must be couched in another painful Perhaps: perhaps both. I have resorted to minor compromises as a result. Translation is an art of compromise.

It hardly needs to be stated that meanings and associations of words differ from language to language. To paraphrase a child's riddle: When is a garden not a garden? Answer: When one garden is in eighteenth century Turkestan and the other is in twentieth century Britain. Climate, geography, custom, distance, time: they stand like stern guardians against total fidelity.

All one can hope, as versifier, is to convey some taste of what was thought long ago, and to introduce an old poet new to the English language. I am proud to have done so.

At the same time, I must take my leave by apologising for many failings in the task. But I was the one who was there, ready, willing and – to some extent at least – able!

BRIAN ALDISS

Glossary

Abdal
A person with one of the degrees in the Sufi order; abdals take the fifth place in the hierarchy of Sufi saints.

Abu Bakr Siddiq
The first Caliph after the Prophet Muhammad.

Ali
Ali ibn-i Abi Talib, also known as Imam Ali, the fourth Caliph and the first of the Twelve Imams (d. 661).

Ali-un-Naqi
The tenth Imam (d. 868).

ana'I-Hak wa mina'I-Hak
"I am Hak (the Truth) and I am from Hak (God)", a phrase mentioned by Hallaj Mansur, one of the earliest Sufis which was misinterpreted by mullahs. When he said: "I am Hak", he meant he reached the Truth and became one with God; mullahs of the time thought he meant he was God. Mansur was killed.

Awlia
Saint.

Baba Zuryat
A Sufi saint of the Middle Ages in Central Asia.

Bahauddin	A Sufi saint and father of Mawlana Jalaluddin-i Rumi.
Belqis	Queen of Sheba.
Bismillah	The short form of "Bismi'llahi'r-rahmani'r-rahim" which means "In the name of God the Compassionate, the Merciful"; it is used at the beginning of an action or a task.
Buraq	The horse which the Prophet Muhammad rode when ascending to Heaven.
Chin Machin	China and beyond.
Dajjal	A legendary personage in Islam due to appear on the Last Day with an ass having ears one touching the earth, the other reaching Heaven.
Duldul	The name of the horse of Imam Ali.
Father	The name of a famous lover in Persian literature who in love with Shirin; their love was the subject of long poems by a number of poets.

Fatima	The daughter of the Prophet Muhammad and the wife of Imam Ali.
Hajjaj	The name of a famous political figure known for his cruelty who became governor of Iraq (694–718).
Haman	The grand-vezir of the Pharaoh; he is mentioned in the Koran.
Hamdu Ii'llah	"Thank God."
Hindustan	India.
Husayn	The third of the Twelve Imams (d. 680).
Illallah	"(No one) but God."
Imam Askar	The eleventh Imam (d. 874).
Imam Ja'far	The sixth Imam (d. 765).
Imam Riza	The eighth Imam (d. 818).
Israfil	An angel according to Islam who reads the decision of God on the "Protected Panel", where good and bad deeds of people are

111

written, and plays the trumpet on Judgement Day.

Jamshid	The name of a legendary king of Persia famous for his crystal bowl in which he could see the world.
Kowsar (Kawsar)	The name of a river in Paradise.
Kul huwallah	The beginning of a verse from the Koran meaning "Say He is God …"
Kyzylbash	Persians.
Lukman (Lokman)	A legendary figure who could cure every illness.
Mahdi	The twelfth Imam (see Sahib-Zaman).
Majnun	The name of the famous lover and hero of the Eastern romance who was in love with Leyla and because of his love he went insane and wandered on the top of mountains and in deserts according to some stories.
Muhammad Baqir	The fifth Imam (d. 731).

Muhammad Taqi	The ninth Imam (d. 835).
Musa Kazim	The seventh Imam (d. 799).
Nasr-I Sayyar	A famous commander of the Muslim army (d. 748).
Nawruz (Nowruz)	The first day of spring (21st March); the name of the festival on this day.
Omar	The second Caliph.
Osman	The third Caliph.
Qaf Mountain	The mountain thought to surround the world binding the horizon on all sides.
Rabbana	"Our Lord."
Rustam	The hero of Shahnameh, the Book of Kings by Persian poet Firdawsi; Rustam is regarded as a symbol of strength.
Safa and Marwa	The name of two hills near the court of Kaaba in Mecca, the distance between which is traversed seven times during pilgrimage.

Sahib-Zaman	The twelfth Imam, who according to Shi'is disappeared and will reappear on the Last Day.
Sajdah	Prostration during the Muslim prayer.
Shaddad	The name of a tyrant in Arab folklore.
Shebli (Shebli)	A famous Sufi of 9th–10th century.
Shimr	The person who killed Husayn, the third Imam in a battle in Karbala.
Shirvan Khan	The Sultan who ruled Azerbaijan in the 15th century.
Sirat Bridge	According to the religion of Islam, the bridge from this world to Paradise which is more slender than a hair and sharper than a sword crossed only by the virtuous.
Sufi	1. A Sufi following the Islamic mysticism. 2. A religious man who has received the blessing of an important religious figure among Turkmens ('Sofi' in Turkmen);

such a Sufi does not necessarily have a religious or any other education.

The Forty	Forty men who opposed the Prophet Muhammad first and later followed Him and became holy men.
The Four Companions	Abu Bakr, Omar, Osman, Ali.
The Seven	Also called Seven "Incomparables" or "Afrad" who occupy the fourth place in the hierarchy of saints.
The Three Hundred (Leaders)	The three hundred chiefs or "Nukaba" who take the eighth place in the hierarchy of saints.
The Twelve Imams	Ali, who is regarded by Shi'is as the only successor of the Prophet Muhammad, and his descendants whose names we read in the poem "The Twelve Imams".
Ummah	A member of the community of the same religion i.e Islam; followers of the Prophet Muhammad.
Varqa and Gulshah	The name of two lovers in Eastern literature who died without being

able to get married and were revived by God afterwards.

Veys-al-Karani — A companion of the Prophet Muhammad.

Yazid — An Umayyidi Caliph (642–683) who is blamed for the massacre of Karbala where the third Imam, Husayn and his children were killed.

Zayn-al-Abidin — The fourth Imam (d. 714).

Zemzem — The well in the court of Kaaba in Mecca.

Zengi Baba — Also known as Zengi Ata, one of the earliest Sufi saints of Central Asia.

Zulfiqar — The sword of Ali.

9 780007 482757